Contents

KU-506-956

Karate

Kathy Galashan

Published in association with The Basic Skills Agency

Hodder & Stoughton

A MEMBER OF THE HODDER HEADLINE GROUP

Acknowledgements

Cover: Telegraph Colour Library

Photos: p 3 Retna Pictures Ltd; pp 6, 13, 17, 19 Hulton Getty; p 9 Telegraph;
p 23 Popperfoto, p 25 Corbis

The author would like to thank Terry Daly and Lascelles James for their help.

Every effort has been made to trace copyright holders of material reproduced in this book. Any
rights not acknowledged will be acknowledged in subsequent printings if notice is given to the
publisher.

Orders; please contact Bookpoint Ltd, 39 Milton Park, Abingdon, Oxon OX14 4TD. Telephone:
(44) 01235 400414, Fax: (44) 01235 400454. Lines are open from 9.00–6.00, Monday to
Saturday, with a 24 hour message answering service.
Email address: orders@bookpoint.co.uk

British Library Cataloguing in Publication Data
A catalogue record for this title is available from the British Library

ISBN 0 340 77518 1

First published 2000
Impression number   10 9 8 7 6 5 4 3 2 1
Year   2005 2004 2003 2002 2001 2000

Copyright © 2000 Kathy Galashan

All rights reserved. No part of this publication may be reproduced or transmitted in any form
or by any means, electronic or mechanical, including photocopying, recording or any
information storage and retrieval system, without permission in writing from the publisher or
under licence from the Copyright Licensing Agency Limited. Further details of such licences (for
reprographic reproduction) may be obtained from the Copyright Licensing Agency Limited, of
90 Tottenham Court Road, London W1P 9HE.

Typeset by GreenGate Publishing Services, Tonbridge, Kent.
Printed in Great Britain for Hodder and Stoughton Educational, a division of Hodder Headline
Plc, 338 Euston Road, London NW1 3BH, by Redwood Books, Trowbridge, Wilts

Terry is a karate teacher.
He has been practising karate for 25 years.
He has won competitions
and has been a British champion.

He is going to talk to Lee.
Lee wants to defend himself in school
and on the streets.
He has seen karate on TV and in films.
It looks exciting.

1   Why do Karate?

Lee   I think I want to learn karate,
but I don't know much about it.
There are lots of different sports
I could do.
Should I choose karate?
What can I get from it?

Terry   Karate is like many things.
You get out of it what you put in.
If you put in the practice
it can help you in lots of ways.
And it's great fun.
I think people want
to feel good about themselves.
That's why all sorts of
men, women, girls and boys
go to classes.

Karate helps to develop balance.

Karate will help you
build up your fitness.
Karate develops balance
and a sense of awareness.
Awareness means you know
where others are and what they are doing.
It will help you control your temper
and focus on what is important.

2   What is Karate?

Lee   Can you tell me something about karate?
          What is it?
          Where did it come from?

Terry   Karate is a martial art.
          It's fast.
          It's powerful.
          It's beautiful.

          It is a way of fighting,
          an art of self-defence.

          Karate started in Okinawa.
          The Japanese made it popular
          all over the world.

          Martial art means 'art of war'.
          Karate means 'empty hands' in Japanese.
          Most karate is fighting with empty hands,
          without using weapons.

Two students demonstrate a karate move.

Lee   So is karate all about fighting, then?

Terry   Not really.
        The art of self-defence is
        not getting into fights.

        Karate is about learning not to fight.
        When you are sure of yourself,
        you don't need to fight.
        You learn to defend yourself
        and attack an opponent
        but you know when to use your skills.
        Self control is a major part of karate.

        I have been doing karate for 25 years.
        In all that time
        I have only had a street fight once.
        I made sure I won.

Lee   If you don't use weapons,
how do you attack your opponent?

Terry I use all parts of my body as weapons.
Believe me, a foot, a knee,
a hand, an arm, an elbow,
shoulders and head can all do real damage.
The most common weapons are hands and feet.
That's what you learn to use first.
Just think of all the different ways
you can use a hand.
You can make a fist.
You can use the side of the hand.
You can use a hand like a spear
with fingers pointing forwards.
Most important is the kiai.
That's the karate shout,
a powerful shout from the stomach.
A kiai in a dark street will make
any attacker think twice.

3   Finding a Karate Class

Lee   So how do I find a class?

Terry   You can find classes
from your local library or sports centre.
There is a national body, the EKGB,
which has lists of all clubs.

Check that the teacher belongs to the EKGB.
Make sure the teacher is insured as well.
Then you are covered
if you get hurt in training.

To begin with, just go along
and try out a class.
If you are going to stay,
you will need to buy a karate suit.

Lee   Are all classes run the same?

Terry   There are different karate styles
and they each follow their own way.
I think the most important thing
is the teacher rather than the style.

In martial arts the teacher is called Sensei.
You learn by following the Sensei
so you need one you trust
and who is serious about karate.

4 What Happens in a Karate Class?

The place where the class is held
is called the dojo.
Dojo means 'training hall' in Japanese.
It's important to treat the dojo
and the people in the dojo with respect.
That is why we bow
at the beginning and end of the session.

A class starts with warm-ups and stretches.
Then you focus on some basic techniques.
Everybody has to learn basic stances.
These are standing positions.
Then there are the moves.
Kicks and punches are ways
of attacking your opponent.
Blocks teach you how to stop an attack.

Karate students.

There is often a part of a class
that concentrates on kicks and punches.
You practise kicking and punching a pad.
You can build up your strength and power
without hurting anyone.
You learn to kick and punch
with your mind as well as your body.
That's what gives a kick power.

Then the Sensei chooses the kata or form.
This is a series of fighting moves
which last about a minute.

You learn kata
because they help focus the mind.
They teach you to concentrate.
They also build your strength
and improve coordination.
They build your awareness
of your surroundings.
That is really important in karate.

5   Sparring

Lee   What about fighting another person?
You make it sound
as if you do it on your own.

Terry First you have to know
how to attack
and how to defend yourself.
That is what you practise on your own.
But then there is a chance
to pit yourself against another person.
Working with another person is sparring.
This is the part I really enjoy.
Everything comes alive
when you are face to face
with another person.
Then the kicks and punches have a target.
What you do depends
on your sparring partner.
You learn to read other people.
You use your awareness and focus
to react and defend yourself.

Lee So what is the point of sparring?
Do you actually hit your partner?
It sounds as if it could be dangerous.
Is it dangerous?

Terry In sparring the main aim
is to hit the other person
in a controlled way
and to block their attack.

Contact can and does hurt.
The karate I do is,
what we call, semi-contact.
That means you don't hit your partner
with full force.
You control the power of the attack.
That is semi-contact karate.

Two members of the British Karate Team in action.

In my style, you can aim at the head
but only make light contact.
The rest of the body is a target
for controlled contact.
Different styles have different rules.

The more you train
the better your sparring becomes.

Grace and skill are displayed in karate practice.

6   Gradings

Lee I've heard about black belts.
How do you get one
and why are they special?

Terry As you learn
you can take tests.
These are gradings.
Students prepare for a grading
by learning kata
and some basic moves,
kicks and punches.
Then there are karate words
you need to know.
The basics all have Japanese names
and you need to learn those.
At a grading you have to show
what you can do.
If you are good enough you pass.
You work your way through the grades.
Each time you pass
you get a different coloured belt.

The final grade is a black belt.
If you train really hard
you can get a black belt
in three years.
Then you are a 1st Dan.
However, you don't stop learning.
When you have a black belt,
that's when the real training starts.
There are 10 Dan
and the 8th, 9th and 10th Dan
are master grades.
So you can see there is a long way to go.

7   Competitions

Lee   What about competitions?
            What are they like?

Terry   Competitions are very exciting
            and a lot of fun.
            You can see top class karate
            and learn a lot.
            It's a chance to test yourself.
            There are local, national
            and international competitions.
            At local level, clubs get together
            and put forward their best people.
            There are competitions for kata.
            Each competitor performs a kata.
            and a judge gives marks out of 10.

The English Council National Championships.

Then there is competition kumite or sparring.
Two contestants face each other on the mat.
First they bow.
The referee starts the first round.
It lasts about two minutes.
Each person kicks, punches and attacks.
Each person tries
to block the attack or move away.
It's fast and powerful
and it's controlled.
The air rings with kiai
as opponents attack.
The referee awards points for a hit.
The winner is through to the next round.

Each karate style holds its own competitions.
In these, everybody you spar with
fights in the same style.
The competitions I find really exciting
are the open competitions.
There you meet new opponents
with different styles.

Two contestants bow to each other to show respect.

Lee   Karate sounds great.
I'd like to give it a try.
But it sounds very serious
and I'd have to practise a lot.

Terry You're right.
It is serious.
It gives you the knowledge to hurt people
but it also gives you the discipline
to use that knowledge.
Don't forget it's fun too.
Good luck with your karate and enjoy!

Glossary of Terms Used

Dojo A training hall.

Grading In karate there are a series of tests.
They let you show how good you are.
The tests are called gradings.

Karate A fighting art. It is one of the martial arts.

Karate Style There are many different styles in karate.
Each one has a different way of perform-
ing moves. The rules are different too.
Some allow full strength attacks.
Some allow controlled attacks.

Kata A sequence of fighting moves that you learn.

Kiai A shout used in karate when you attack
an opponent.

Kumite Controlled fighting with an opponent
in karate.

Sparring Controlled fighting with an opponent
in karate.

semi-contact karate Karate styles where the attack on the
opponent is controlled. The kicks and
punches are not delivered at full strength.

Finding Out More

To find a club near you contact the EKGB:
English Karate Governing Body
53 Windmill Balk Lane
Woodlands
Doncaster DN6 7SF

Telephone: 01302 337645
e-mail: info@ekgb.org.uk.
www.EKGB.org.uk

Magazine: *Traditional Karate*